Life's Little Lessons on

Inspirational Quotes and Insig

John C. Maxwell

eagle

Guildford, Surrey

Copyright © 1994 by John C. Maxwell

1530 Jamacha Road, Suite D, El Cajon, California 92019
The right of John C. Maxwell to be identified as author of this work has been asserted by him in accordance with the Copyright, Design and Patents Act 1988.

First published by Honor Books, P.O. Box 55388, Tulsa, Oklahoma 74155.
This edition published 2000 by Eagle Publishing (IPS) Ltd, PO Box 530, Guildford, Surrey GU2 4FH.

British Library Cataloguing in Publication Data. A catalogue record for this book is available from the British Library.

All rights reserved. No part of this publication may be reproduced or transmitted in any form or by any means, electronic or mechanical, including photocopying, recording or any information storage and retrieval system, without either prior permission in writing from the publisher or a licence permitting restricted copying.

In the United Kingdom such licences are issued by the Publishers Licensing Society Ltd, 90 Tottenham Court Road, London W1P 9HE.

Typeset by Eagle
Printed by Interprint Ltd, Malta
ISBN No: 0 86347 359 8

Introduction

Leaders are readers! Even thousands who don't read widely, read wisely. They clip out articles and file quotes for future use. For thirty years this has been my practice.

Over the years, I have often been asked to share my quote collection. *Life's Little Lessons on Leadership* is my attempt to fulfil those requests for material, specifically on the subject of leadership. Long ago, I learned that if you want to quote like a leader you must note like a leader. In this book, you will find some great material – so start filing!

John Maxwell

Life's Little Lessons on . . .

Leadership is influence.

John Maxwell

Leadership

This is my favourite definition of leadership. It's a simple, straightforward, one-word description that places leadership within everyone's reach. All of us can exercise a certain degree of influence on someone, at some point, in some place. Leadership isn't about titles, positions or flowcharts. It's about one life influencing another.

Life's Little Lessons on . . .

Character is power.

Booker T. Washington

Leadership

The first lesson we must each learn is that broad leadership is built from deep character. An infrastructure of great character is essential to support great conduct. The trust and involvement of our followers will be parallel to the level of our own character.

Life's Little Lessons on . . .

Use power to help people. For we are given
power not to advance our own purposes, nor to make a
great show in the world, nor a name.
There is but one just use of power,
and it is to serve people.

George Bush

Leadership

George Bush was right. We abuse our power when we utilize it for self-gain. One of the buzzwords of the 1990s was the word 'empower'. It simply means to give your power away. This is what people are longing for their leaders to do. This truth is echoed by Jesus in Matthew 20:26 '... whoever wishes to become great among you shall be your servant ...'.

Life's Little Lessons on . . .

Failure can be divided into those who thought and never did and into those who did and never thought.

Reverend W.A. Nance

Leadership

Someone once told me the world has two kinds of people: thinkers and doers. They then said, 'The thinkers need to do more, and the doers need to think more.' I have always tried to do both – reflect and act. When I have combined the two, I have greatly reduced the odds of failure.

Life's Little Lessons on . . .

Leaders must be close enough to relate to others, but far enough ahead to motivate them.

John Maxwell

I have always believed this principle. It beautifully combines the necessity of both relationship and vision. I must live with the people to understand them and earn their trust. However, I am only their 'buddy' if that's all I do. To be a leader, I must live with God and move with Him beyond where the people are. If they are to follow me, I must be ahead of them.

Life's Little Lessons on . . .

> Leadership is the capacity
> to translate vision into reality.
>
> Warren G. Bennis

Leadership

Most of us learn the hard way that leadership is not merely having a vision. Anyone can dream. Effective leadership is knowing how to lay down the action steps for yourself and the organisation so that the vision can be realized. This requires us to be practical and to understand the process along the way.

Life's Little Lessons on . . .

You manage things;
you lead people.

Grace Murray Hopper
Admiral, U.S. Navy (retired)

Leadership

I must have articulated this principle a hundred times during my years as a pastor. People don't want to be managed, organized, stereotyped, tagged or filed. That's what you do with things in an office. People are dynamic and must be led through love and relationship.

Life's Little Lessons on . . .

A man must be big enough
to admit his mistakes, smart enough
to profit from them, and strong
enough to correct them.

Leadership

One of the least talked about prerequisites for leadership is a strong sense of personal security. Without it, I sabotage myself and my organization. With it, I can handle mistakes with perspective, and have the ability to admit them, profit from them and correct them.

Life's Little Lessons on . . .

I don't know the key to success,
but the key to failure is trying
to please everybody.

Bill Cosby

Leadership

One of the weaknesses of many of today's leaders is our compulsion to take surveys. It happens in politics, and it happens in churches. A leader must go beyond being a people-pleaser to being a God-pleaser. If our need for the people's affirmation exceeds our need for God's affirmation, we're in trouble. Leadership sometimes means doing what's unpopular.

Life's Little Lessons on . . .

You are the same today that
you are going to be in five years
from now except for two things:
the people with whom you associate
and the books you read.

Charles 'Tremendous' Jones

Leadership

I read this statement by Charlie Jones years ago, and I've become more convinced of its truth as time goes by. If we plan to become great, we must determine to expose ourselves to great books and great people. Their input will influence our growth more than anything else. Choose both wisely.

Life's Little Lessons on . . .

No matter what size the bottle,
the cream always came to the top.

Charles Wilson
President, GE

Leadership

Pastoring in the Midwest, I quickly learned that people are somewhat like fresh milk from a cow. At first glance, it all looks the same. But eventually, the cream rises to the top. Similarly, you'll find that given time, the 'movers and shakers' naturally rise to the top. Simply watch and wait.

Life's Little Lessons on . . .

A ship in a harbour is safe but that is not what ships were built for.

Leadership

We've all seen this statement on a plaque or poster somewhere. What a great reminder it is that safety, security and survival are not meaningful goals for our lives. If we're going to get anywhere, we're going to have to risk venturing into the unknown. Life is about adventure, not maintenance.

Life's Little Lessons on . . .

You can have brilliant ideas,
but if you can't get them across,
your ideas won't get you anywhere.

Lee Iacocca

I discovered this truth as I observed my staff attempting to cast a vision to the people in their departments. Ideas alone can't harness a group of people. We can only move to accomplish a goal when the vision is cast clearly, creatively and consistently.

Life's Little Lessons on . . .

Asking 'who ought to be the boss?'
is like asking 'who ought to be the tenor
in the quartet?' Obviously, the man who
can sing tenor.

Henry Ford

Leadership

I love the simple, unpretentious logic of Henry Ford. He cuts through the red tape of human politics, suggesting that leadership isn't a matter of tenure, or title, but ability. The appropriate question is, 'Who can get the job done?'

Life's Little Lessons on . . .

Nothing great was ever
achieved without enthusiasm.

Ralph Waldo Emerson

Leadership

I am an attitude nut. I just happen to believe that an enthusiastic attitude places a leader above his peers, opens his mind to creativity and provides motivation to his people. 'Enthusiasm' is taken from two root words: 'en' and 'theos', meaning 'God within'. If we have God living on the inside of us, we ought to be enthusiastic!

Life's Little Lessons on . . .

The best executive is the
one who has sense enough
to pick good men to do what he
wants done, and self-restraint
enough to keep from meddling
with them while they do it.

Theodore Roosevelt

Leadership

I have always tried to lead my staff this way: I select and salary my team based upon ability and productivity. When I place a leader in a position that fits his/her abilities, it is apparent in the overall quality of their work. That done, I leave them to reach the goals we've set in whatever way they choose. I don't care so much how they get to the goal, as long as they reach it!

Life's Little Lessons on . . .

> The single most important factor in determining the climate of an organization is the top executive.
>
> Charles Galloway

Leadership

Everything rises and falls on leadership. Once a leader has been directing an organization (or church) for two years or more, the personality, atmosphere and problems of that organization are a result of his leadership. When you see him, you see his organization.

Life's Little Lessons on . . .

You must live with people
to know their problems, and live
with God in order to solve them.

P.T. Forsyth

Leadership

This truism combines two very important ingredients for a leader. A leader is called to stand in the gap between the people and God. We must be close enough to the people to represent them (their needs and struggles) before God. At the same time, we must be close enough to God to represent Him (His answers and directions) before the people. This is the key balancing act before us.

Life's Little Lessons on . . .

Reportedly IBM's Tom Watson was asked if he was going to fire an employee who made a mistake that cost IBM $600,000. He said, 'No, I just spent $600,000 training him. Why would I want somebody to hire his experience?'

Leadership

Tom Watson's response provides insight to leaders who are tempted to let a staff member go after a mistake or failure. If their mistake was not immoral or fundamentally undermining to the direction of the organization, we might do well to keep them. Why not view it as a learning experience and consider it an investment in the future?

Life's Little Lessons on . . .

Failure is the opportunity
to begin again, more intelligently.

Henry Ford

Leadership

Once again, Henry Ford's simplicity strikes me. Failure was never final to him, nor was it fatal. Like his contemporary, Thomas Edison, he expected failures on the way to success. It was all part of the learning process. He allowed failure to tutor him, then he continued on down the path that much smarter and wiser.

Life's Little Lessons on . . .

> Show me a thoroughly satisfied man,
> and I will show you a failure.
>
> Thomas Edison

Leadership

I find it terribly difficult to understand a person who is so satisfied with their present accomplishments that they have no desire to risk attempting something new. There is nothing wrong with spiritual contentment with our possessions and resources, but each of us should carry to our grave a holy dissatisfaction with our achievements.

Life's Little Lessons on . . .

> I will have no man work for me
> who has not the capacity
> to become a partner.

J.C. Penney

Leadership

I have heard many single women say they won't date a man who isn't a potential marriage partner. They don't want to waste their time with unproductive emotional entanglements. J.C. Penney looked at employees the same way. He looked for the raw ability in all of them – the capacity to rise in the organization. If necessary, it is wise to create a position for those kind of people when you find them!

Life's Little Lessons on . . .

Here lies a man who knew
how to enlist the service
of better men than himself.

Andrew Carnegie's Tombstone

> **Leadership**

I am drawn to Carnegie's humility, as well as his talent. He didn't try to do it all, or to own it all. He once said, 'I owe whatever success I have achieved, by and large, to my ability to surround myself with people who are smarter than I am.' He knew his own limitations, but that only spurred him on to find associates who didn't have the same ones.

Life's Little Lessons on . . .

Luck is the residue of design.

Branch Rickey

Leadership

People talk a lot about good luck and bad luck. I believe, however, that Branch Rickey was right. Very few outcomes in this cause and effect world are due to chance. Someone has said, 'Good luck is what happens when opportunity meets preparation.'

Life's Little Lessons on . . .

All glory comes
from daring to begin.

Eugene F. Ware

Leadership

To begin a task is usually the toughest step. Indeed, the journey of a thousand miles begins with a single step, but I've found *that* step keeps most people stationary. The fear of attempting something big immobilizes them. This is why beginning is half the battle, and why all glory comes from daring to begin.

Life's Little Lessons on . . .

Don't spend a £1.00's worth
of time on a £10 decision.

Leadership

I try to invest the appropriate amount of time and mental energy into every decision I make. Visualize a scale: on one side is the weight of how much the decision will cost. On the other, how much it will benefit. Balance each decision's potential benefit with its actual cost.

Life's Little Lessons on . . .

> Nothing gives one person so much advantage over another as to remain always cool and unruffled under all circumstances.
>
> Thomas Jefferson

Leadership

Poise comes through maturity. When we get it, and can keep it under pressure, we will have a decided advantage over others. Panicking usually has a negative effect on a situation, but remaining calm and cool enables us to think and act more intelligently. Make it your ambition to never panic.

Life's Little Lessons on . . .

The moment you stop learning,
you stop leading.

Rick Warren

Leadership

Leaders are learners. Once a person feels they have a firm grasp on all the answers, they have stopped being teachable and will soon cease leading. Their thoughts and methods will become dated, and eventually stale. Good leaders are hungry for learning, all the way to the grave.

Life's Little Lessons on . . .

A person that is successful
has simply formed the habit
of doing things that unsuccessful
people will not do.

Leadership

Whatever business field you may have chosen, success will follow you if you will consistently do the things and provide the services that others refuse to do and fail to provide. This makes for outstanding leadership and creates a demand for you and what you do.

Life's Little Lessons on . . .

You can't build a reputation
on what you're going to do.

Henry Ford

Leadership

Our reputation is obviously constructed from our track record, not our intentions. As I travel, I meet pastors and businessmen from all over the country. Many of them know the right principles, talk the correct language and lay the proper plans. Unfortunately, it takes more than that to build a dynamic church or a profitable business. Success is all about what we've produced, not what we've planned.

Life's Little Lessons on . . .

If you want to succeed you should strike out on new paths rather than travel the worn paths of accepted success.

John D. Rockefeller, Jr.

Leadership

It's amazing to me that the levels of Olympic competition at the turn of the twentieth century are now the levels at which junior high school students compete. Why is that? During the last 100 years, athletes have invariably discovered new ways to run faster, jump higher and throw further. Success, therefore, has meant not merely doing what previous champions have done, but pioneering new methods.

Life's Little Lessons on . . .

> You cannot push anyone
> up the ladder unless he is
> willing to climb a little.

Andrew Carnegie

Leadership

No one can succeed for you. Success isn't a gift to be given away. Believe me, I have tried many times to 'jump start' one of my staff, just to help them make it beyond where they might have gone alone. Some responded and rose to the challenge. Others, despite my optimism, were unable or unwilling to climb a step up the ladder.

Life's Little Lessons on . . .

People support what
they help create.

Leadership

I'm convinced that the surest way to establish a sense of ownership among your constituency is to involve them in the creative process, all along the way. You might be able to reach a goal faster on your own, but when you get there you will be just that – on your own. Slow down, and take your people along.

Life's Little Lessons on . . .

It's what you learn after you
know it all that counts.

John Wooden

Leadership

John Wooden has been there. Here's a coach who could have easily assumed he knew it all. It's at that point, however, that the greatest lessons and most profound discoveries are found. Someone once said: 'We only learn what we already know.' When we get beyond a superficial understanding of an idea or concept is when the truth really sinks in.

Life's Little Lessons on . . .

A good leader is a guy who can step on your toes without messing up your shine.

Leadership

I've seen some of the best pastors and business executives in the country at work. They all seem to have the keen ability to speak the truth, to lay out the imperatives and to communicate the marching orders to their people. At the same time, they do so with such warmth and understanding, with such humour and sensitivity that no one feels pushed. They actually like the experience and feel they are better for it.

Life's Little Lessons on . . .

> We are what we repeatedly do, excellence then is not an act, but a habit.
>
> Aristotle

Leadership

Success is not an event. It is an ongoing process we engage in, time and time again. Aristotle says it in a profound way. Anyone can succeed once or twice. And anyone can fail or lose a battle or two along the way. What we must focus on is the habit of excellence; practising success, repeatedly, day after day.

Life's Little Lessons on . . .

Eagles don't flock – you have
to find them one at a time.

H. Ross Perot

Leadership

You've probably noticed this too. Unlike most birds, eagles don't fly in flocks. They don't simply fit in. They don't conform to the activities of their own kind. You cannot find them in huge clusters. They are flying alone, ahead of and higher than the other birds. Leaders are like eagles.

Life's Little Lessons on . . .

A man who has to be
convinced to act before he
acts is not a man of action.

Georges Clemenceau

Leadership

I can easily lose patience with people whom I continually have to persuade before they will make a move. People of action don't need a pep talk every time their organization needs to take a risk. I'm not suggesting we don't plan, but men of action often embrace the method that Tom Peters made popular: 'Ready, Fire, Aim.'

Life's Little Lessons on . . .

> Be a yardstick of quality.
> Some people aren't used
> to an environment where
> excellence is expected.

Stephen Jobs

Leadership

Stephen Jobs, the young founder of Apple Computers, understood as well as anyone what it takes to build excellence into people. He knew that most people don't pursue excellence naturally. Pioneering a new corporation, he recognized that he had the opportunity to set a standard from the very beginning. Ultimately, he understood that this could only take place if he became the example of the quality he desired. He had to be the yardstick for excellence.

Life's Little Lessons on . . .

A man who wants to lead
the orchestra must turn his
back on the crowd.

Leadership

This little word picture is pregnant with meaning. If a man wants to lead the orchestra, he must first make a solitary decision. He cannot drift along with the crowd, nor can he pay attention to the crowd's response to his leading. He must remain focused and be willing to stand alone. He must give himself to the few who are co-operating with him, not the masses who are looking on. Finally, even if he yearns for the crowd's applause, that cannot be his goal. His goal must be to lead his orchestra with excellence. The applause is a by-product.

Life's Little Lessons on . . .

Congealed thinking is the forerunner of failure
. . . make sure you are always
receptive to new ideas.

George Crane

Leadership

I don't have to remind you that we live in a world of fast-paced change. We laugh at the fact that the US Patent Office nearly closed down towards the end of the nineteenth century, because many felt that nothing new could be invented. Those who lead the pack today are those who are not only open to change, but to the new paradigms – whole new ways of looking at established facts. It was the Swiss who invented the digital watch, but because their own watchmakers weren't open to a new idea – the Japanese have capitalized on it ever since.

Life's Little Lessons on . . .

It's OK to lend a helping hand –
the challenge is getting
people to let go of it.

Leadership

When something is freely offered, for long enough, it is human nature to become dependent upon it. This is the reason behind the cry for welfare reform in the US. People get comfortable with the helping hand, and soon believe they can't live without it. Good leadership empowers people by providing the resources they need to get started, but the goal is to teach them how to be resourceful themselves.

Life's Little Lessons on . . .

Being in power is like being
a lady. If you have to tell
people you are, you aren't.

Margaret Thatcher

Leadership

I love this quote from Margaret Thatcher. Any time our leadership is not obvious enough to those around us that it requires an explanation, we're in danger of losing it. If you must continually remind people that you are in control – someone else is likely assuming that role. Leadership should appear natural and be evident to all.

Life's Little Lessons on . . .

I recommend you to take care
of the minutes, for the hours
will take care of themselves.

Lord Chesterfield

Leadership

Sometimes, we miss the forest for the trees, and other times we miss the trees for the forest. When we only see the 'big picture' and fail to see to it that the 'minutes' are dealt with appropriately, we may miss accomplishing our big-picture goals. If we take care of the little things, we can build on that foundation and eventually the hours will fall into place.

Life's Little Lessons on . . .

An important question for leaders:
'Am I building people, or building my dream and using people to do it?'

John Maxwell

Leadership

Jack Hayford taught me something years ago. He said, 'Our goal isn't to build a big church – but to build big people.' If we invest in people, and develop them into mission-driven disciples, we will see our dream for the church accomplished. People quickly ascertain whether we are building them or using them.

Life's Little Lessons on . . .

Learn to say 'no' to the good
so you can say 'yes' to the best.

Leadership

This is the battleground where I fight most often. I can easily distinguish between good and bad. Yet with my disposition, which wants to do everything, accomplish everything and say 'yes' to everything, I need accountability to choose between good and best. I have a 'hatchet committee' that helps me say 'no' to the good things along the way.

Life's Little Lessons on . . .

Outstanding leaders appeal
to the hearts of their followers,
not their minds.

Leadership

If you reflect on the most well-remembered political leaders in American history. you'll find men who were able to grip the hearts of the people: Lincoln, Roosevelt, Kennedy, Reagan. It's not about partisanship. It's about the ability to cast a vision, to empathize, to spark hope, to speak to the heart. It's not that these leaders didn't use logic; they just travelled beyond logic, to win the hearts of their audience.

Life's Little Lessons on . . .

> No man will make a great leader who wants to do it all himself, or to get all the credit for doing it.

Andrew Carnegie

Leadership

Leadership, by definition, cannot be a one man show. If I don't possess the humility and desire to enable me to praise others and give them credit for their success, I'll be severely handicapped in my leadership. If my ego is so big that I insist on the applause, attention and affirmation, potential partners will leave me alone; and I will end up with only what one person can accomplish.

Life's Little Lessons on . . .

Leadership is not wielding authority –
it's empowering people.

Becky Brodin

Leadership

Too many leaders make the mistake of thinking when they reach the top, it means they can use their position and power to force certain behaviours from their subordinates. We've all made the statement, 'If *I* were in charge – things would be different . . .' However, leadership is not about a power trip, but about giving power to the people under you. It's about giving them the tools they need to do the job.

Life's Little Lessons on . . .

Every great institution is the lengthened shadow of a single man. His character determines the character of his organization.

Ralph Waldo Emerson

Leadership

Every organization reflects its leader. There would be no compassionate organization called The Salvation Army if not for William Booth. There would have been no Methodist Awakening if not for John Wesley. The modern missionary movement would not exist without William Carey. God doesn't look for masses, or even for committees, when He wants to do something – He looks for a leader.

Life's Little Lessons on . . .

The most effective leadership is by example, not edict.

Leadership

Nearly 90 per cent of how people learn is visual. It's what we see. Another 9 per cent of our learning is verbal, or what we hear. About 1 per cent is through our other senses. This alone explains why effective leadership is more caught than taught. People need to see a sermon, more than hear it, to really embrace it. A leader's credibility and his right to be followed are based on his life, as much as his lip.

Life's Little Lessons on . . .

Whistler's Law: You never know who's right, but you always know who's in charge.

Leadership

I've chuckled at the truth of this 'law' more than once. There are indeed, times when it's difficult to determine who is right. In fact, it may be an issue of subjective opinion in some cases. However, determining who's in charge is not nearly as difficult; just watch the people. When a tough decision needs to be made, who do they look to? Who do they trust? That's the person in charge.

Life's Little Lessons on . . .

The most pathetic person
in the world is someone who
has sight but has no vision.

Helen Keller

Leadership

This is my favourite statement made by Helen Keller, a woman who was blind and deaf all of her life. She said this in response to the question: 'What could be worse than being born without any sight?' Vision is non-negotiable for anyone who wants to succeed. It is the blueprint on the inside of a leader, before he ever sees the plan on the outside.

Life's Little Lessons on . . .

If a man knows not what harbour he seeks,
any wind is the right wind.

Seneca

Leadership

This quote from Seneca is indicative of how so many people live their life. Not knowing what long-term direction they are headed for, they bounce around like a ball in a pinball machine. They live reactive lives based on what happens to them, rather than pro-active lives based on what values are in them. They live their lives 'by accident' rather than 'on purpose'.

Life's Little Lessons on . . .

It is only as we develop others
that we permanently succeed.

Harvey S. Firestone

In a word, the goal of a leader is to leave a 'legacy'. He wants to leave behind something permanent after he dies. He wants to have improved the lives of people in some corner of the world, or better yet, see them engaged in a cause that counts. This doesn't necessarily mean fame or wealth. It simply means people who continue in a mission because he has developed them.

Life's Little Lessons on . . .

The highest compliment leaders can receive is the one that is given by the people who work for them.

Leadership

To me, success is being respected by those who are closest to me. I want to display integrity to those who see all my warts and wrinkles. I want to have the admiration of my family and colleagues, the people who see me day in and day out. It's easy to be honoured and esteemed by those who are far away and seldom seen. I want to be a hero at home.

Life's Little Lessons on . . .

It isn't the people you fire
who make your life miserable,
it's the people you don't.

Harvey Mackay

Leadership

Throughout my ministry, I've been fascinated by the words Jesus spoke in John 15. Specifically, where He talks about pruning the vine so that the branches could continue to grow. I've met scores of pastors and leaders who are afraid to 'prune' when it comes to their staff. They think it would not appear very 'Christian'. Quite the contrary, the concept is not only biblical, but if we don't practise it in our organizations, someday it may come back to haunt us.

Life's Little Lessons on . . .

Today a reader –
tomorrow a leader.

W. Fusselman

Leadership

One of the principles I've always tried to practise is to be well-read. I believe every meeting I enter without the preparation of good information is one where I can't easily assume my leadership role. Knowledge is power. As the leader, I must know more about the options in front of us, than my boards and committees. Reading helps my leading.

Life's Little Lessons on . . .

The essence of leadership is a vision you articulate clearly and forcefully on every occasion. You can't blow an uncertain trumpet.

Theodore Hesburgh

Leadership

I'll never forget hearing the 'vision' of the Pepsi company a number of years ago: 'The taste of Pepsi-Cola on the lips of everyone in the world.' What a huge, overwhelming vision – yet how precise, measurable and pointed it was. Everyone in the company knew it, and was harnessed to achieve it. Our vision must be heard until our people can embrace it.

Life's Little Lessons on . . .

Leadership development is a
life-time journey – not a brief trip.

John Maxwell

Leadership

I believe this now more than ever. About fifteen years ago, I thought I had a handle on leadership. No doubt I did understand some significant leadership principles. But the more I grow, the more I recognize that my own leadership development will take a lifetime. It's not something we can pick up from a weekend conference. We must commit to it.

Life's Little Lessons on . . .

The test of leadership: Turn around, and see if anyone is following you.

Leadership

This is the acid test of leadership. If you want to evaluate your own leadership, look at the people following you. Is anyone following? What kind of people do you attract? Does your vision compel people to follow? Are they committed to the vision? This is a simple series of questions every leader should ask himself.

Life's Little Lessons on . . .

If you pay peanuts,
expect to get monkeys.

Leadership

I believe in having a staff that is 'lean and mean' rather than 'fat and sassy'. As my last church grew, we were able to do so without adding any new staff over a long period of time. The reason? I paid my pastoral staff well, and I got the best. Because I paid them well, I was able to maintain a strong core, and as we grew they assumed multiple responsibilities – and they didn't have to work for peanuts.

Life's Little Lessons on . . .

It is wonderful when the
people believe in their leader:
but it is more wonderful when the
leader believes in the people!

Leadership

It is difficult to say which must come first: the leader believing in his people or vice versa. However, I do know this: if a leader begins to believe in his people, it is only a matter of time before both occur. The fundamental step a leader must take is to believe in his people and communicate it to them. Don't ever settle for merely impressing them.

Life's Little Lessons on . . .

If a leader demonstrates competency, genuine concern for others, and admirable character, people will follow.

T. Richard Chase

Leadership

T. Richard Chase distills the basic components that followers look for in a leader. Are they competent? Do they really care for people? Do they possess strong character? Everything else is icing on the cake. Followers can endure a wide spectrum of differences in their leaders, but these three elements are non-negotiable.

Life's Little Lessons on . . .

There is no security on this earth –
only opportunity.

Leadership

I think I first heard this statement as a quote from a general in World War II. This world we live in does not offer any lasting security. It can't. What it does offer is trials, challenges and a whole lot of opportunity. Our security can only be found in our obedience to God's call on our lives.

Life's Little Lessons on . . .

My responsibility is to be a
supervisor, not a super-worker.

Fred Smith

Leadership

Sometimes when we experience growth in our organization, we forget that our role as a leader must evolve, too. The larger our organization grows, the less we can do by ourselves. We must commit ourselves to the task of oversight, or we will be overworked. While we must always model work, our chief task is empowering others to work.

Life's Little Lessons on . . .

Vision is the art of
seeing things invisible.

Jonathan Swift

Leadership

One of my favourite stories of possessing vision is about Walt Disney. Because Walt had passed away before the Grand Opening of Walt Disney World, Mrs Disney was asked to appear on the stage at the opening ceremony. When she was introduced to come to the podium and greet the crowd, the master of ceremonies said to her, 'Mrs Disney – I just wish Walt could have seen this!' Mrs Disney simply replied, 'He did!'

Life's Little Lessons on . . .

> Pay now, play later;
> play now, pay later.
>
> John Maxwell

Leadership

I learned this simple truth from my dad. It's helped me to discard the notion of immediate gratification hundreds of times over the years. If I choose to pay the price for my dreams now, I'll enjoy the rewards of those dreams later. However, if I choose to play now, I may not have the opportunity for reward later. I'll be too busy paying the price.

Life's Little Lessons on . . .

Failure to prepare is
preparing to fail.

Mike Murdock

Leadership

Oh, I have found this to be true! I want to be prepared for every event that I face. That's why I read. That's why I listen to tapes. It's why I study. It's why I dialogue with staff. I want to reduce the 'surprise factor' as much as possible – life itself presents enough surprises, even for the thoroughly prepared. When I fail to prepare in one area, I set myself up for potential failure in other areas as well.

Life's Little Lessons on . . .

> A great man is always
> willing to be little.

Ralph Waldo Emerson

Leadership

Great people have little use for fame or notoriety; they are consumed with productivity, not image. They do not feel the need to project their self-worth to anyone. They are content when the moment calls for them to be little, ordinary or common – as long as the goal is achieved.

Life's Little Lessons on . . .

As a rule . . . he (or she) who has the most information will have the greatest success in life.

Disraeli

Leadership

We've all heard it before: knowledge is power. Because there is doubtless truth to this axiom, I consume as much information as I possibly can, in a variety of subjects relevant to me and my work. I have noticed that success follows the person who brings something to the table when the meeting begins; they are well-read and well-prepared. They never come across as ignorant in any subject.

Life's Little Lessons on . . .

Having confidence that
if you have done a little
thing well, you can do
a bigger thing well too.

Storey

Leadership

Life is full of graduations. In each stage of our journey, God has planned where we will either pass or fail the quiz life has presented. Not only does God promise greater opportunities when we have proven to be faithful in the little things, but we also gain confidence when we've been successful in them. Remember, young David graduated from the bear, to the lion, to the giant.

Life's Little Lessons on . . .

Dreams are the touchstones
of our character.

Henry David Thoreau

Leadership

All across the country, as I meet leaders, one question I enjoy asking them is: 'What is your dream?' You can tell a lot about a man's character by the substance and size of his dreams. They speak volumes about his motives, priorities, values, purposes and goals.

Life's Little Lessons on . . .

The most important thing about
having goals is having one.

Geoffry F. Abert

Leadership

Simply possessing a goal will put you in a higher league than most of your peers. I remember J.C. Penney once said: 'Show me a stockclerk with a goal, and I'll show you a man who'll make history. Show me a man without a goal, and I'll show you a stockclerk.' Goals make the difference between dreaming and doing.

Life's Little Lessons on . . .

Some people change jobs,
mates and friends, but never
think of changing themselves.

Leadership

We live in a generation consumed with changing exteriors. We've bought into the notion that if we just can change the people, circumstances and environment around us, we can solve our problems. Most of the time, however, the issue lies within us. God doesn't hold us responsible for what happens *to* us, but for what happens *in* us.

Life's Little Lessons on . . .

If you see a snake, just kill it.
Don't appoint a committee on snakes.

H. Ross Perot

Leadership

So much needless red tape exists in many organizations. I hate red tape. I agree with Ross Perot when it comes to the 'snakes' of life. If we know what the 'bottom line' is, then we can clear any obstacle that prevents that goal. Often, we don't need any further research or discussion; we simply hide behind it, because it looks like positive action. Look for ways to radically solve problems. Activity does not always equal accomplishment.

Life's Little Lessons on . . .

> Lord, when I am wrong, make me willing to change; when I am right, make me easy to live with. So strengthen me that the power of my example will far exceed the authority of my rank.

Pauline H. Peters

Leadership

What a fitting note to conclude with. This disarming petition forces me, as a leader, to adjust my heart as well as my head. When all is said and done, I want the life I model to speak louder than all the degrees, ranks and titles I may have earned. After all, when my journey is over, I want my leadership to be who I am, not merely what my job description says I do.

About the Author

Dr John C. Maxwell was the senior pastor of one of America's largest churches for 14 years. He is also known across the world as a motivator, encourager and equipper of leaders. He has conducted leadership seminars nationally and internationally, and is the founder and director of INJOY, Inc., a leadership development company. He is the author of numerous books, with well over half a million copies in print.

Life's Little Lessons on Relationships
Insights and Wisdom on Building Relationships

'No man is an island' said John Donne, and despite some people's denial of the fact, sooner or later everyone realizes that human beings aren't designed to 'go it alone'. If that were not the case, solitary confinement might be considered a reward rather than a punishment!

Doctors Leslie and Les Parrott have made the study of relationships their life's work and the insights they have gained are recorded here to help all of us who struggle with living and working with other people!

As well as their own wisdom, the authors pass on advice from well known people from history and give various 'points to ponder' on making and improving relationships.

On the road between the homes of friends, grass does not grow.
NORWEGIAN PROVERB

EAGLE PUBLISHING
0 86347 361 X